G000151416

The Pocket Book
of Tutankhamun
Egyptian Museum in Cairo

Text by Abeer el-Shahawy
Photographs by Farid Atiya

The Pocket Book
of Tutankhamun
Egyptian Museum in Cairo

Text by Abeer el-Shahawy
Photographs by Farid Atiya

Published by Farid Atiya Press
©Farid Atiya Press
P.O. Box 75, 6th of October City, Giza, Cairo, Egypt
Fax. : 0020-2-8331-745; www.faridatiyapress.com, e-mail : atiya@link.net

First edition, 2005
Colour Separation by Farid Atiya Press
Printed and bound in Egypt by Farid Atiya Press
Dar el-Kuteb Registration 5388/2005
ISBN 977-17-2106-2
Front cover : Tutankhamun on a papyrus raft; page 55;
Back cover : Detail of the ornamented chest, pages 103 - 107;

List of Illustrations

8 & 9. Gold mask of Tutankhamun

Gold, Semi-Precious Stone, Glass Paste; 18th Dynasty, reign of Tutankhamun 1336 - 1346 BC; H. 54 cm; Upper floor, room 3; JE 60672;

This stupendous mask of King Tutankhamun is made of solid gold, and ornamented with lapis lazuli, turquoise, carnelian and coloured-glass paste. It is a masterpiece indeed, and one of the highlights among the treasures. The mask was found covering the mummy's head and shoulders, and weighs 11 kilos, it shows the king, as a young man in his teens. He is wearing the *nemes* royal headdress, with a cobra and a vulture over the forehead, symbols of the unification of Upper and Lower Egypt.

The eyebrows and eye lines are inlaid with lapis lazuli, and the eyes themselves are inlaid with obsidian and white quartz. The red dot at the corner of each eye adds a touch of realism to the mask. The king is wearing a false funerary beard with a curved end, which is again inlaid with lapis lazuli. The chest is covered with a large usekh multi-tiered pectoral, also inlaid with lapis lazuli as well as turquoise and carnelian, and culminating at the sides with falcon heads.

The elongated face, arched eyebrows, large pierced ears, and lines on the neck are all traces of Akhenaten's Amarna art, wrought here with great realism and beauty. The rear side of the mask reveals the *nemes* headdress, gathered in a braid on the shoulder; and the hieroglyphic inscription bears texts explaining the religious significance of the mask. The gold and lapis lazuli associated the deceased with the god Re, whose flesh is of gold, and hair of lapis lazuli. The facial features of the mask are identified with divinities mentioned in Spell 151b of the 'Book of the Coming Forth by Day' ('The Book of the Dead'), to enable the deceased a safe passage to the realm of Osiris in the hereafter. The protection of the head of the deceased was one of the important concerns in ancient Egypt; the mask provided a permanent substitute for the head in case of damage.

In the Old Kingdom, facial features were painted on top of the mummy bandages that covered the faces. The earliest masks, dating from the First Intermediate Period, are hollow masks carved of wood, made of two pieces that are held together with pegs. Some are of 'cartonnage', modelled over a wooden core. The masks of the New Kingdom Period are more sophisticated and elaborate than before, and by this time, the making of permanent face coverings ran parallel to the mummification process. Finally, in Roman times, the masks evolved into flat portraits covering the faces of mummies.

The semi-precious stones used in this mask, and elsewhere, were symbolic. In ancient times, every stone was believed to possess certain magical powers, lapis lazuli, or *khesbed* in ancient Egyptian, considered to be the most precious, after gold and silver, because of its special blue like the colour of the heavens. It was imported from Syria and Palestine, and was used right from the beginning of Egyptian history. The red of carnelian represented dynamism and power, and the blue-green colour of turquoise symbolised growth.

9

Gold was used to attain immortality because of its sun-like brilliance and its resistance to corrosion. It could be hammered and melted into thin sheets to cover the body like skin. Gold was related to the afterlife, and intended as a means of acquiring the flesh of the gods.

In his Amarna letter, the King of Mittani, Tushrata, describes the gold of Egypt 'as abundant as the dust on the ground'. The ancient Egyptians first found gold in Coptos, 35 km north of Luxor. It was described as 'the gold of Coptos' and quarried from a site near Wadi Hammamat and Wadi Abbad.

Nubia, whose name may have been derived from the word for gold *nbw*, was the best source of this precious metal. In Lower Nubia, called *wawaat*, gold was present at Wadi Alaki. In Upper Nubia, then called Kush, it was found at Soleb and Semnah. There were fortresses in Nubia to control the commerce of the gold, which was presented as a tribute to Egypt.

In preparing the raw material, fire was used to crack the quartzite stone, which was then pounded, and later washed over a sloping table in order to separate the metal from the quartz. Finally, the gold was melted and formed into ingots.

Some occupational titles were connected with gold production, from 'The Gold Washer', 'Scribe Reckoner of Gold', to more elevated titles like 'Overseer of the Gold Lands' and 'Overseer of the Treasury'.

The metal was worked in workshops that were attached to royal palaces or temples. One of the goldsmith's techniques was 'cold-hammering', which was used for the preparation of gold sheets. It was also worked hot, the molten gold poured into molds of various shapes. The 'lost-wax' method was also used. Here, the desired shape was formed from wax, which was encased with clay and then heated, to melt the wax; leaving a hollow to be filled with molten gold. Later, the clay would be removed and the gold item, finished and polished.

13. Ka statue of Tutankhamun

Wood coated with bitumen; H.198 cm, W. 53 cm; Upper floor, gallery 45, JE 6070;

Carved of wood, this life-size statue is partly gilded, and is one of two statues that stood at the entrance of the burial chamber, as though guarding it. The entrance was blocked by a stone wall, which ancient robbers broke through, entering the chamber, and stealing some of the treasures. They were later caught, however, and the stone wall was restored by funerary priests, who put their seals on the wall. The pair of statues depicts the king and his *ka*, or double, which was thought to represent the attributes that designate character and temperament. The king is shown with his *khat* headdress, which signified both rejuvenation, and the nocturnal side of the solar cycle. The headdress reveals the ears, which are shown pierced, as in Amarna art. The other *ka* statue shows the king wearing the *nemes* headdress.

A gilded bronze royal cobra lies over the forehead for protection. The eye lines and brows are inlaid with gilded bronze; and the eyes themselves, with white quartz and obsidian. The king wears a large pectoral and a pendant necklace. Bracelets and armbands of gold leaf also adorn the wooden statue.

In one hand the king is holding the *hedge* mace, as the traditional weapon of a victorious king; and in the other, a staff in the form of a papyrus plant, which symbolises youth and freshness. He wears the starched, pleated kilt that was the fashion of the period. The buckle on his belt displays Tutankhamun's cartouche, and contains the title *neb kheprw re*, 'the lord of existence of the god Re'. The cartouche on the other statue contains the name *Tut ankh Amen*, 'the living image of the god Amen'.

Wearing gilded bronze sandals, the king is standing in the traditional posture with the left foot advancing, as though striding forward.

The king is shown here with black skin, the colour having been achieved by coating the wood with bitumen. Also, as the colour of the Nile mud that flooded the land and gave it fertility every year, black signified resurrection and the continuity of life. In addition, this colour was associated with the underworld, and sometimes the skin of Osiris was represented as black, emphasising the belief that, after death, the king would personify Osiris, god of the hereafter. Black skin, moreover, recalled the Nubian guardians, who were known to be powerful, shrewd and fierce; and would therefore frighten any intruder in the tomb, giving added protection to the funerary treasures.

Egyptologists initially believed that Tutankhamun was either poisoned or died of tuberculosis. An x-ray of the mummy, however, made in Liverpool in 1969, showed a wound beneath the left ear, suggesting that probably a brain haemorrhage, resulting from this wound, had led to the king's death. However, whether he was murdered or was the victim of an accident has not been determined with certainty.

Shortly after the burial, robbers broke into the tomb and took with them some of the light, but valuable objects, leaving the tomb in disorder. Officials and priests later tidied up the antechamber.

The death of Lord Carnarvon in 1923, shortly after the discovery of the treasure-filled tomb, caused speculations about 'the curse of the pharaohs'.

16 & 17. Inner gold coffin of Tutankhamun

Gold, Semi-Precious Stone; L. 187.5 cm; Upper floor, room 3; JE 60671;

This anthropoid coffin was the innermost of three coffins, which were placed one inside the other, then placed in turn within a larger rectangular quartzite sarcophagus with a granite lid. This coffin is made of solid gold and weighs 110 kg, while the other two coffins are made of gilded wood. The second one is displayed alongside this, the innermost coffin. The third and largest coffin now contains the mummy and is inside its sarcophagus in Tutankhamun's tomb in the Valley of the Kings at Luxor.

When discovered, the coffins rested inside each other so tightly that it was impossible to insert one's little finger between them. Moreover, the funeral libation poured over the coffins, during the funerary rites, had stiffened and solidified, like cement. Freeing them, therefore, caused damage to much of the decorative and inlay work, although this was later restored.

The coffin shows the king wearing the *nemes* royal headdress, and the cobra and vultures over the forehead personify the two protective deities of the unified Upper and Lower Egypt. The portrait of the young king here, with features showing the influence of Amarna art, resembles the mask. The eyebrows and eye lines are inlaid with lapis lazuli, but the eyes are missing. The king wears his funerary curved false beard. Around his neck is a double-tiered *shebyu* necklace, formed by threaded gold discs. A multi-tiered *usekh* pectoral covers his chest. The king is shown in the Osiride pose, with arms crossed over the chest. He is holding the *heka* crook, symbol of power; and the *nekhekh* flail, symbol of authority. Wide bracelets adorn the wrists.

The cobra and vulture spread their wings to protect the king's body, holding the *shen* amulet as a symbol of continuity and infinity.

The goddesses Isis and Nephthys are represented in the form of the *djerty*, two women with outspread wings, offering protection to the deceased. As sisters of Osiris, and his two main mourners; they perform the same service for the deceased king, who is associated with Osiris.

17

19. Coffin of Tutankhamun's internal organs

Gold, semi-precious stone; H. 39 cm, W. 12 cm, D. 12 cm; Upper floor, room 3; JE 60688;

This miniature anthropoid coffin is one of four, which contained the internal organs of the king: the stomach, intestines, lungs and liver that were removed from the body at the time of mummification. These organs were embalmed and wrapped in linen, then placed in the four miniature coffins, that then went into the alabaster, canopic jars. On the lids of these jars are images of the king's head. Particular care was taken with the organs, as these jars were in turn placed in an alabaster canopic chest, which was found in the gilded wooden chest in the treasury of the tomb, adjacent to the burial chamber.

The king is shown in the traditional manner, wearing the *nemes* royal head-dress, with a cobra and vulture, the protective deities of unified Upper and Lower Egypt, on the forehead. The eyebrows and eye lines are inlaid with lapis lazuli; and the eyes themselves are inlaid with white quartz and obsidian. A curved false beard is attached to the chin. He wears two small *shebyu* neck-laces, and a large *usekh* pectoral. The king is represented in the Osiride form, with arms crossed over the chest, and holding the *heka* crook, symbol of power, as well as the *nekhekh* flail, symbol of authority. He is also wearing wide gold bracelets.

Two wings envelope the torso and the entire coffin is inlaid with semi-precious stones such as lapis lazuli, carnelian and turquoise as well as with coloured-glass paste in a *rishi,* or feathered design.

The hieroglyphic column in the middle shows the prayers of the goddess Nephthys and the god Hapy, who was the protector of the lungs, one of the Four Sons of Horus protecting the jars containing the viscera, together with the other three deities Dwamutef, Qebehsnuef, and Imsety.

The back of the coffin shows the *nemes* gathered in a braid; and underneath, the claws of the vultures are holding the *shen* amulet, which is a symbol of everlasting continuity and infinity.

One of the other three coffins shows that the cartouches were altered, indicating that these miniature coffins were made for another person; but due to Tutankhamun's premature death, the names were altered and used to store his organs.

23 & 25. Canopic shrine

Gold and wood; H. 198 cm, L. 153 cm, W. 122 cm; Upper floor, gallery 9;
JE 60686;

Found in the treasure room of Tutankhamun's tomb, this gilded wooden shrine stood against the east wall, facing the door of the burial chamber. It contained a smaller alabaster canopic chest that in turn housed the four canopic jars, containing the viscera. Inside these jars were the four miniature coffins with the internal organs of the king.

The shrine is placed over a sledge, and surrounded by a canopy formed of four pillars that support the roof, which features a cavetto cornice. The upper part of the roof is decorated with protective cobras, inlaid with coloured-glass paste, and their heads are surmounted with solar discs.

Four goddesses surround the shrine, spreading their arms in a protective manner. The head of one is turned, showing alertness and a readiness to attack any intruder, as an added measure for the safety and protection of the chest. The turned head breaks the tradition of frontal poses seen in the older statuary, due to the influence of Amarna art, which is also evident in the representation of slim necks and naturalistic bodies. The goddesses wear headdresses from which their hair descends; and their identities are revealed in the hieroglyphic inscriptions on the heads. They are the goddess Isis, who carries a throne on her head; the goddess Nephthys with a house and a basket on hers; the goddess Selket, identified with the burning heat of the sun, bears the scorpion on her head; and the goddess Neith of the city Sais in the north-west Delta has two bows on her head. These four goddesses were associated with the Four Sons of Horus, and together the eight formed a protective group to guard the internal organs of the deceased. In addition, these eight deities are mentioned in protective religious formulas on this shrine, which also bears the king's cartouches. The roof of the shrine features a cavetto cornice, and the upper part is decorated with protective cobras inlaid with coloured-glass paste, their heads surmounted by solar discs.

The goddesses are wearing close-fitting dresses, and the naturalistic style of their bodies, again shows the influence Amarna art. The goddess Selket, who personified the scorpion, was worshipped, in order to prevent its fatal stings. She is the protector of the god Qebehsenuef, the hawk-headed Son of Horus. Her cult existed as early as the First Dynasty.

Another deity associated with the scorpion was the goddess *Shed*, described as 'the saviour, who bestowed protection against the scorpion stings'. *Shed* was depicted on stelae at a chapel in the workmen's village in Tell el-Amarna. In addition, seven scorpions protected Isis from her enemies.

The title *sa srkt*, the Guardian of Selket, was one of the titles given to the funerary priests, present in the scenes of funeral processions depicted on the walls of the Theban nobles tombs. Examples include the Tomb of Amenemhat at Gournah (TT 82) and Montuherkhopshef at Draa Abu el-Naga (TT20).

The sledge on which the shrine rested was meant to facilitate its movement. It also had a religious significance as a symbolic connection to the sun god Atum and the Four Sons of Horus, who were believed to raise the deceased to heaven on a sledge.

27. Pectoral of the sky goddess Nut

Gold, semi-precious stone; H. 12.6 cm, W. 14.3 cm; Upper floor, room 3;
JE 61944;

This shrine-shaped pectoral shows the goddess Nut with outstretched arms and wings. The upper part is surmounted with a cavetto cornice. The cartouches give the names of King Tutankhamun, but show some alteration and modification, having probably belonged to another king and reused for king Tutankhamun. On the other hand, the alteration may be the correction of a mistake.

Every evening, Nut was believed to swallow the setting sun and then give birth to it every morning. These acts are depicted on the ceilings of several tombs in the Kings Valley and in many temples. The fact that the sun made another journey through the underworld was not contradictory to that belief, as Nut's body was the route of the stars, and she was one of the funerary deities referred to in the Pyramid Texts. In the New Kingdom Period, representations of the deceased were shown under Nut's protection, assuring his rebirth, just as the sun was newly born each day. Nut afforded protection among the imperishable stars in her body, and as such, was depicted on the underside of many coffin lids to give such assistance to the deceased.

A member of the Heliopolitan Ennead, Nut is mentioned in Spell 548 of the Pyramid Texts as the celestial cow who suckles the king and takes him to herself in the sky. The goddess is, in fact, often represented as a woman, whose na-

ked body is arched over the earth. In addition, in Spell 306 of the Coffin Texts, she performs the swallowing of the deceased, who is identified with Re.

The deceased sought magical protection for his soul by the use of amulets and jewellery, just as he sought physical protection through mummification. The most typical funerary jewellery was an attempt to gain help and influence by magical means.

29. Pectoral of the sky goddess Nut as a vulture

Gold, semi-precious stone; H. 12 cm, W. 17 cm; Upper floor, room 3; JE 61943;

Some 143 pieces of jewellery were found in Tutankhamun's treasures, and the whole collection amounts to 3,500 pieces. Some of the jewellery was found on the mummy, and other pieces were found inside the various chests and boxes placed inside the tomb. This pectoral was found in a chest, surmounted by the god Anubis in the tomb treasury, adjacent to the burial chamber.

The hieroglyphic signs on the rear side of this pectoral associate the vulture here with the sky goddess Nut, who is in turn associated with 'Isis that protect Osiris and Horus and accordingly will protect the mummy', as indicated in Chapter 157 of the 'Book of the Dead'.

Another vulture goddess called Nekhbet, is often related to kings and kingship. One of her earliest appearances holding the *shen* sign was on the Second Dynasty stone vase of Khasekhemwy from Hierakonpolis, which was the cu

29

center of that goddess. Other goddesses are also represented as vultures like the goddess Mut, wife of the god Amen and a member of the divine Theban triad.

32 & 33. Pectoral of Osiris, Isis and Nephthys

Gold, semi-precious stone; Upper floor, room 3; JE 61946;

Tutankhamun's treasures include 26 pectorals and those worn during his life show signs of wear. This pectoral, which appears to have been worn was also found in the Anubis chest in the tomb treasury. It is shaped like a shrine, featuring a cavetto corniche at the top and surmounted by two cobras with vultures' wings. Under the cornice, is a frieze of lotus flowers with a cobra wearing the solar disc at both sides.

At the right side of the pectoral is a cobra wearing the Red Crown of Lower Egypt, and two wings framing a *shen* sign. It lies on a basket with a checker design. Although this cobra represents the goddess Wadjet, the protective deity of Lower Egypt; the text beside it gives the name of the goddess Nephthys. The left side of the pectoral features a vulture wearing White Crown, which is flanked by two feathers, recalling the *atef* crown. It stretches its wings to protect the shen sign, and is resting on a basket similar to the one on the right side. Here too is the vulture goddess Nekhbet, the deity of Upper Egypt, and an accompanying text mentions the name of Isis.

In the centre, Osiris is shown in mummy form, wearing the atef crown and a large pectoral; holding the *heka* and *nekhekh* scepters. Osiris here represents the king himself, who would be associated with Osiris after death and resurrected in his realm in the hereafter. The text beside runs: *nb neheh, heka djet, neter nefer, nb ta djeser,* 'The lord of eternity, ruler of everlasting, the good god, lord of the holy land'.

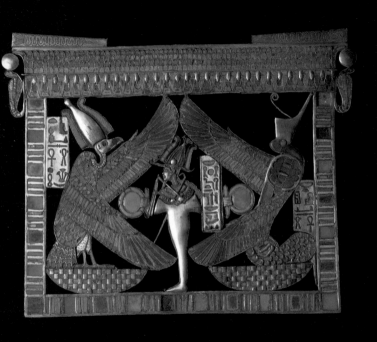

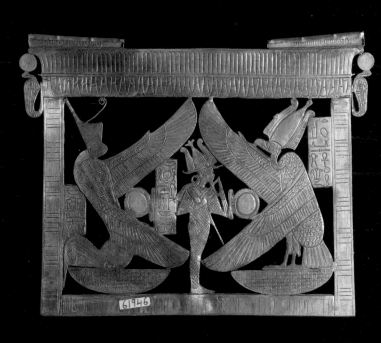

33

35. Pectoral with a winged scarab

Gold, silver, silica glass; H. 15 cm, W. 15 cm; Upper floor, room 3; JE 61884;

Comprised of composite motifs, the upper part of this pectoral shows the figure of the king, accompanied by the falcon-god Reherakhty, whose head is surmounted by a solar disc. In addition, there is the ibis-headed god Thot, whose head is surmounted by both the crescent moon and the full moon.

Inside a solar barque is the left *udjat* eye of Horus, flanked by two cobras, each wearing a solar disc on its head. The *udjat* is the eye of the falcon god Horus with its characteristic marking beneath. The word *udjat* means 'the perfect' it belongs to Herwer, who was worshipped at Kom Ombo. An early creator god, 'his right eye was the sun and his left eye was the moon'. During the mythical struggle between the god Horus and his enemy Seth, the left eye of Horus was plucked out, but later restored by the god of wisdom Thot. Horus, the son of Osiris, later brought his father back to life by giving him this eye. This offering of the eye was an alternative to food offerings, and the lunar and solar *udjat* are mentioned in Chapters 140 and 167 of the 'Book of the Dead.' The *udjat* eye pendant contained great protective power, imbuing the bearer with particular protective qualities.

The barque represented the nocturnal journey of the sun. It is shown here carried by a winged scarab, which holds the *shen* sign of eternity. Scarab beetle is the *scarabaeus sacer.* It became a symbol of new life and rebirth because the beetle lays eggs in a ball of dung. The ancient Egyptians equated the hatching

of the eggs with the rise of the 'newly born' sun. The scarab god Kheperi was a creator god, sometimes represented as a man with a scarab head or as a scarab in a boat held by Nun, god of the primeval ocean. The scarab, which emerged from balls of dung, was associated with creation. In the Pyramid Texts, Kheperi was referred to as a sun god, 'he who is coming into being'.

37. Earrings with duck heads

Gold, glass; L. 10.9cm; Upper floor, room 3; JE 61969;

This pair of earrings is the most beautiful of the four pairs discovered in Tutankhamun's treasures. The ducks with outstretched wings form a circle and their feet hold the *shen* sign. The head is made of translucent blue glass and the wings are fashioned in cloisonné. Under the duck hang gold and blue glass beads with five cobra heads. These earrings show a great aesthetic sensibility, and ducks held a specific erotic symbolism. The statues of the king never showed him wearing such earrings, however.

Earrings were worn in Mesopotamia and Nubia earlier than in Egypt where they started to appear at the end of the Second Intermediate Period, at the end of the 17th Dynasty. During the New Kingdom Period, earrings became common, and were worn by both sexes although women are more frequently shown wearing them. Kings were never represented with earrings although the statues and some of the mummies show pierced ears.

37

39. Collar of the Two Ladies

Gold, semi-precious stones, coloured glass; Upper floor, room 3

Discovered between the bandages on the chest of Tutankhamun's mummy, this piece is called the *nebty* collar or the Collar of Two Ladies.

It shows a cobra flanking a vulture with outstretched wings. The piece and its counterpoise were made using the cloisonné technique, inlaid with hundreds of pieces of semi-precious stones and coloured-glass. Glass and faience possessed magical properties for the ancient Egyptians as they could be transformed from a dull white substance or silica, lime, alkali into a glimmering material. The *nebty* was a royal title as early as the fourth king of the First Dynasty King Djet, and signifies the cobra and vulture as the two protective deities of Upper and Lower Egypt. The cobra is a protective deity called Wadjet, who represented Lower Egypt in the kings' titles. She was described as the *wrt hekaw* 'the great of magic'. She was also associated with the eye of Re, protecting the sun god. In addition, she was represented guarding the gates that divided the hours of the underworld.

The vulture is Nekhbet, is goddess of el-Kab, in Upper Egypt. One of her feet ends with the *shen* sign of infinity. *Shen* means to encircle, to last forever; and the cartouche is a modification of this sign.

41 - 43. Cosmetic box

Gold, silver, semi-precious stones; H. 16 cm, W. 8.8 cm, D. 4.3 cm;
Upper floor, room 3; JE 61496;

This double cartouche-shaped box was used as a container for cosmetics or ointments. The face on the box shows Tutankhamun as a child, indicated by the lock of hair at the side of his head. The cobra over the forehead, signifies royalty. The hands are placed over the chest, and the king is holding the royal insignia the *heka* crook and *nekhekh* flail.

On his head is the solar disc representing god Ra, flanked by two cobras, with *ankh* signs hanging from each; the king is squatting over a sign symbolising the *heb* feast. Another solar disc, on top of the lid, is flanked by two feathers.

The other sides of the box show the king variously wearing the Blue Crown; again squatting over the *heb* sign, holding the *heka* and *nekhekh* scepters in one hand, and resting the other hand on his knee. Similar solar discs having the above-described decoration as its counter part on the other side exist over his head.

One of the king's faces is black, symbolising the underworld as well as the resurrection and continuity of life, black being the colour of the Nile mud that flooded the land and gave it fertility every year. Moreover, black is one of the colours associated with Osiris, who is sometimes seen with black skin, there-

41

43

fore, emphasising the belief that the king, after his death would personify Osiris, the god of the hereafter.

A representation of Heh, the god of eternity, is seen on the third side of the box. Like the king, he is squatting over the *heb* feast sign and holding two palm fronds, which represent the promise for a million years of life for the king, whose cartouches are represented beside him. Over his head, we see the name *neb kheperw re* enclosed by palm fronds.

The box's base is made of silver, and decorated with the *ankh* and *was* symbols of life and prosperity.

Indeed, the box shows great elegance, refinement and a fine artistic sense, as well as a high standard of skills that involved casting and hammering techniques.

45 & 47. Necklace with a pectoral in the form of a solar boat

Gold, silver, semi-precious stone and glass paste; Overall Length 44 cm, W. 11.5 cm, H. 6.3 cm; Upper floor, room 3; JE 61885;

This outstanding pectoral came from a wooden box in Tutankhamun's tomb treasury. Suspended from a necklace, it features the scarab god Kheper inlaid with lapis lazuli, and holding a solar disc with his front legs and the *shen* symbol with his back legs. Two squatting baboons are also represented at the top of the two shrines represented here. The baboon heads are surmounted with the lunar crescent and lunar disc. This animal was sometimes used to represen

Thot, the god of writing and wisdom, who had a lunar aspect. The baboon was also used in sun symbology. At sunrise, these animals greet the sun with high screams, and by stretching their bodies. They are seen here in a solar boat sailing on the waters of Nun, the primeval ocean, represented as series of zigzag lines inlaid with blue lapis lazuli.

The sides of the pectoral are framed by the *was* sign, indicating prosperity, while on the top is the sign *pt,* hieroglyph for the sky, which is adorned with stars and inlaid with gold and lapis lazuli.

The necklace from which this pectoral hangs shows images of the god Heh, the god of eternity, and over them is the sign signifying the *sed* festival. The necklace also comprises gold and glass beads.

Clearly, jewellery was not only used to signify rank, wealth or social status, as the symbolism it contained had amuletic use. Certain chapters of the 'Book of the Dead' required the provision of amulets as part of the funerary accoutrements. Scarabs, made of various materials, were often used as amulets in jewellery, either strung in bead-form as necklaces, or scattered loose among the bandages. The various types of funerary scarabs also include the winged scarab for protection and the heart scarab, understood to be 'begging the heart not to be a witness against the deceased on the Day of Judgment'. The heart scarab was especially significant as a funerary amulet, in accordance with Chapters 26 - 30 of the 'Book of the Dead'.

49. Head of Tutankhamun emerging from the lotus flower

Painted wood; H. 30 cm; Upper floor, gallery 20; JE 60723;

Carved of wood that is covered with gesso and painted, this piece shows the king's head emerging from a lotus flower. The head is elongated, and this feature, together with the arched eyebrows, slanted eyes and large pierced ears, as well as the lines on the neck, are all characteristics of Amarna art. The lotus flower is depicted on a bluish-green base that represents the water of the Nile where lotus flowers usually profilerated.

The lotus was highly symbolic in Egyptian art and religious beliefs, appearing as one of the two heraldic symbols, the lotus and the papyrus, signifying Upper and Lower Egypt. In this piece, the lotus flower indicates the rejuvenation and the resurrection of the king. According to the Hermopolis theory of the creation of the world, the newly born sun was created from a lotus flower that emerged from the primeval ocean Nun. The lotus, which opened its petals and emerged from the Nile every day symbolised the daily rebirth of the sun. The deceased expected to be reincarnated in different forms in order to circulate the realm of the underworld; taking the form of the lotus flower would guarantee his rebirth as the newly risen sun.

For this reason, scenes of noblemen and women, carrying or smelling the lotus, frequently occur in the mural decorations in tombs. Because it opened under the rays of the sun, the lotus defeated darkness and death.

49

52 & 53. Miniature Effigy of the Pharaoh

Wood; L. 42 cm, H. 4.3 cm, W. 12 cm; Upper floor, gallery 25; JE 60720;

This effigy came from a black rectangular chest in the treasury room, and according to the inscriptions on its sides, was dedicated to Tutankhamun by the scribe and treasury superintendent, Maya. It was wrapped in linen sheets alongside miniature agricultural tools that were made for the *ushabti*, the symbolic answerers who were to serve the king in the afterlife. It shows the king lying on a funerary bed that looks like the mummification table, which is decorated with two lion heads as well as paws and tails. The king is represented wearing the *nemes* royal headdress with the royal cobra over his forehead. His eyes and eyebrows are outlined in black paint and the whites of the eyes are painted in. He is wearing a multi-tiered pectoral, and his arms are crossed in the Osiride posture. His body is wrapped in linen bandages like the mummy shape of the god Osiris. Beside the king are two birds: the *ba* bird with a human head and the falcon, representing the god Horus. The outspread wings of both birds cover the chest of the king.

The symbolism in this piece is very prominent, linking the king with the theme of resurrection and rejuvenation. The two lion gods, called Aker, are identified with the eastern and western horizons. Between them they support the rise of the sun, representing the sun of 'yesterday and tomorrow' and thereby, symbolising eternity.

The *ba* is one of the elements forming the human individual, which is considered as the soul or spirit. The *ba* was thought to return to the mummy and hover over it, reuniting every night with Osiris, who was embodied in the mummy itself. This union enabled the *ba* to be reborn each day among the living. The piece, in fact, symbolises the union of Ra and Osiris in the underworld, where, it was believed, they met in the depths of the darkness each night; and Ra received the power of rebirth from Osiris. At the same time, Osiris was resurrected in the form of Ra.

According to the same theme, Horus, the son of Osiris, became the son of the king, insofar as he had become Osiris. The son would assure a proper funeral procession and burial for the king, protecting him against any enemies that might hinder him in his path. Spell No. 60 of the Coffin Texts refers to the journey made by the deceased, who had become Osiris, and who had to be protected against foes, especially Seth. 'The god is in his shrine, he makes a journey by boat before going down into the necropolis; the boat is pulled straight towards the necropolis; the son whom he loves that is his pious heir, the *sm* priest, the lector priest and the embalmer, act for him; he receives food offerings; he ends in a columned shrine, which is to serve as his protection'.

53

55. Tutankhamun on a papyrus raft

Stuccoed and gilded wood, bronze; H. 69.5 cm, W. 18.5 cm, L. 70.5 cm; Upper floor, gallery 45; JE 60709;

In another piece from the treasury room in the tomb of King Tutankhamun, the king is here seen standing on a flat papyrus boat that is painted green and partially gilded. The prow and stern are both decorated with papyrus flowers.

The king is represented wearing the *deshert* Red Crown of Lower Egypt, with the royal cobra over his forehead. His eyebrows and eyes are outlined in black; he wears a multi-tiered *usekh* pectoral, and is seen striding forward, holding a harpoon to hunt in the Nile. In his other hand, he holds a cord made of bronze to tie up his prey, creatures like the hippopotamus and crocodile. He wears a short pleated kilt and sandals. While the king may have wished to enjoy such a hunting trip in the Delta marshes in the afterlife, the scene bore a religious significance. It symbolised the victory of the king over the evil forces that would cause cosmic disorder. Moreover, it associated the king with Horus, who had spent 82 years fighting Seth, to avenge the murder of his father Osiris. Horus finally won victory over Seth, who had assumed the form of a hippopotamus. The harpooning scenes are also interpreted as a conflict between the fertile valley and the barren desert that threatens to overcome it. Success in the hunt then, meant the victory of the fertile valley over the desert.

The dynamic posture of the statue is such that was rarely seen before the Amarna period. Other influences from Amarna art are the naturalism of the king's face, together with the fleshy breast and abdomen; the slim arms and legs.

This statue was found together with six other royal statues and a group of 27 statues of divinities inside several black wooden chests. All were wrapped in sheets of linen as if mummified, and only the heads were visible. A date mentioning the third year of Akhenaten's reign was recorded on the linen sheets, indicating that those linen sheets had either originally belonged to Akhenaten, or that the statues themselves had belonged to Akhenaten, but had been usurped and modified to be reused for Tutankhamun.

57. Tutankhamun on the back of a leopard

Gilded and painted wood; H. 85.6 cm; Upper Floor, gallery 45; JE 60714;

One of an identical pair, this statue was found in the treasury room of Tutankhamun's tomb, in a black wooden chest containing another 33 statues of the king and of various divinities. The piece is carved of wood and covered by a layer of stucco, before being gilded. It shows the king wearing the *hedjet* White Crown, with the royal cobra over his forehead, his eyebrows and eyes outlined in black. He wears a multi-tiered *usekh* pectoral, a pleated short kilt and sandals. In his right hand, he is holding the *nekhekh* scepter, symbol of authority

and a long staff in his left. He is standing on a rectangular pedestal that rests on the back of a leopard.

What appears simply as a hunting scene also had a religious significance, identifying the golden-skinned king as the sun god Re. The black leopard represents the night sky. The sky swallows the sun, in order to be reborn every morning, out of the body of the sky. The king on the leopard's back shows his domination of the situation, and emphasises his rebirth and resurrection. He is like the sun reborn every day.

Tutankhamun's calm face reveals his confidence in the triumph over death. Meanwhile, the panther is represented with a fierce naturalistic face that adds an air of liveliness and realism.

The influence of Amarna art is again apparent in the naturalism of the king's face as well as in the fleshy breast and abdomen, and the thin arms and legs.

60 & 61. A goddess carrying the King

Gilded and painted wood; Upper floor, gallery 45;

Carved of wood and covered by a layer of stucco, this gilded statue was found in the treasury room of the tomb of King Tutankhamun. It shows the king wearing the *deshret* Red Crown, with the royal cobra over his forehead, his eyebrows and eyes framed in black. He wears a multi-tiered *usekh* pectoral and his body is shown covered in bandages, recalling those of the god Osiris. It shows the king carried by the goddess Menkart, who would help facilitate his journey through the underworld. She is wearing a long straight wig, and a tight pleated dress with geometric motifs. The buckle of her belt shows the *tit* symbol, which is the knotted girdle of the goddess Isis. Described in Chapter 156 of the Book of the Dead as 'red as the blood of Isis, this sign signifies the protection that Isis provided for the mummy.

On the statue's rear side is the *ankh* sign of life and the *sa* sign of protection. Like the previous two statues, this one also shows the Amarna influence in the naturalistic renderings of the two figures.

61

62 & 63. Statue of Ttutankhamun with the Red Crown

Gilded and painted wood; H. 59 cm; Upper Floor, gallery 45; JE 60713;

   This statue was found together with the previous three statues in the treasury room of the tomb. Carved of wood and covered by a layer of stucco, this gilded statue shows the king wearing the *deshret* Red Crown, with the royal cobra over his forehead, his eyebrows and eyes are framed in black. He wears a *usekh* necklace, a pleated kilt and sandals. In his right hand, he holds the *nekhekh* symbolizing authority and in his other hand he holds a staff. Like the other three previous statues, the influence of Amarna art is again apparent in the naturalism of the king's face as well as in the fleshy breast and abdomen, and the thin arms and legs.

66 & 67. Statue of Sekhmet

Gilded and painted wood; H. 55 cm; Upper Floor, gallery 45; JE 60794;

This statue was carved of wood and covered with a gold leaf. It shows the goddess Sekhmet who was one of the healing goddesses who wielded special power, being well versed in magic.

Represented as a lion-headed woman, Sekhmet has a solar disc over her head. She is sitting on a throne wearing a close-fitting dress decorated with geometrical motives. On the side of the throne, the *sematawy* scene is shown, with lotus and papyrus plants tied together; suggesting the country's unification under the throne of Sekhmet. One of her titles was *Sekhmet aat nbt tawy*, 'the great Sekhmet, lady of the two lands'.

The name Sekhmet means 'the mighty one' and was derived from the word *ekhem*, which means power. Her many other titles include: *wrt hekaw*, 'the great of magic', *nbt srdjwt*, 'the lady of terror', *nbt irt*, ' the lady of action'.

Sekhmet was one of the manifestations of the fiery eye of Re. A member of the Memphite triad, she was wife of Ptah and mother of Nefertum. Lions were viewed as magical guardian figures, and many other goddesses were often represented as lionesses, such as the goddesses Pakhet, Tefnut, Hathor, Bastet and Mut. The two lion gods called Akr were identified with the eastern and western horizons, between them supporting the rise of the sun. They represented 'yesterday and tomorrow', thereby symbolising eternity.

67

70 - 72. Throne of Tutankhamun

Wood, gold leaf, silver, semi-precious stones; H. 100 cm, W. 54 cm, L. 6 cm;
Upper floor, gallery 35; JE 62028;

Another of the masterpieces in the Egyptian Museum, this throne was found under the funerary beds in the antechamber of the tomb. It is made of wood and covered with gold leaf, which is inlaid with silver and semi-precious stones like lapis lazuli, carnelian and turquoise, as well as coloured-glass paste. The piece shows great artistry and technical skills. The legs of the throne are in the form of lion's paws, inlaid with lapis lazuli claws. The front legs are surmounted with lion's heads, the eyes inlaid with white quartz and crystal. Originally, a filigree decoration forming the *sematawy* scene of the lotus and papyrus plants, was present between the legs of the throne, symbolising the unity between the north and the south.

The arms of the throne bear other symbols of unification as well as of protection, which is signified in the head of the cobra with the wings of the vulture; the two protective goddesses of Upper and Lower Egypt. The *sekhmety* Double Crown on the cobra head shows the unity of the country: the White Crown is made of silver and the Red Crown, of gold. The wings of the vulture enclose the *shen* sign of infinity; and the king's cartouches as well as the *nsw-biti*, one of his titles as King of Upper and Lower Egypt. In addition, the title on the right of the throne shows the king's original name of Tutankhaten. The name, meaning 'the living image of Aten' was replaced by 'the living image of Amen' following the abandonment of Tell el-Amarna and the return to Thebes, where the cult of Amen and the pantheon of other divinities was restored. The throne, therefore, dates from the earlier years of Tutankhamun's reign when he was still living in Tell el-Amarna.

The footstool, also carved of wood, stuccoed and gilded, features six bows that represent the foes of Egypt, shown as three Asiatic and three Nubian enemies, all under the complete control of the king who would trample over them. The hieroglyphic text includes the phrase *taw khaswt wrw n rtnw kher tbay.k* 'All the great foreign lands of the Retenw (Asiatics) are under your sandals.' The sides of the stool show the bird *rekhyt*, which symbolises the Egyptian populace, together with the sign *nb,* meaning 'all', alongside a star, which means 'to adore'. Together, these words mean that 'the king is adored by all the populace'.

75 - 77. Ceremonial chair

Ebony, ivory, gold leaf, stone, faience; H. 102 cm, W. 70 cm, D. 44 cm;
Upper floor, gallery 25; JE 62030;

This wooden chair was found in the annex of the tomb's antechamber. Inlaid with ebony, ivory and semi-precious stones, the stool is also partly gilded. As a folding stool that, supplied with a back, doubles as a chair; it is a fine example of folding furniture.

The feet of the throne are decorated with ducks heads inlaid with ivory as well as the *sematawy* sign, which is partly damaged.

Chairs were status symbol in ancient Egypt. Some are cushioned and there are stools with concave seats of latticework. Others have slanted or curved backrests, and yet others have straight, flat backrests. The legs are usually of feline design. The seats themselves are, most often, a mesh of linen cords, or woven rush. Some stools have crossed legs and deeply curved seats and others are three-legged.

The upper part of the chair back is decorated with a frieze of royal protective cobras surmounted by a solar disc. In the middle of the frieze is the disc of the god Aten, which is placed above two cartouches that bear the names of that god. A vulture goddess is represented, spreading her wings to protect the king, who would sit on the chair. Under the goddess is a representation of two feathers, together with the *shen* symbol of eternity and infinity. At the extreme right and left, we see the names of the king in his cartouches as Twt ankhaten and

Nebkheprwre. The vertical hieroglyphic inscriptions underneath, giving the titles and new name of the king as Tutankhamun, were added later.

This footstool represents the nine enemies of Egypt as individuals; the enemies here replaced the traditional metaphor of the nine bows. They are depicted with the naturalism that is characteristic of Amarna art. Their facial features reveal their origin as either Asiatics or Africans. One is represented in old age, which is apparent by the wrinkles on his neck.

When the king sat on the chair, he placed his feet on the footstool, signifying that all his foreign foes were under his feet, and, therefore, subject to his authority. The accompanying text here reads as follows: 'All the great foreign lands of the Retenw (Asia) are like one thing under your sandals forever and ever like Re'.

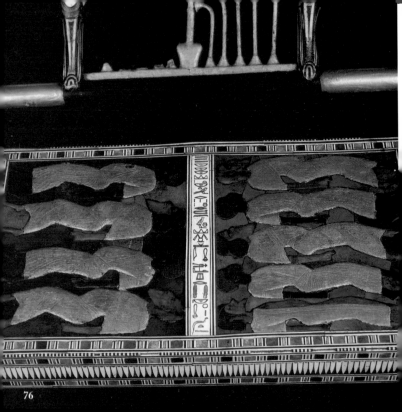

78 - 81. Chair with god Heh

Wood, gold leaf; H. 96 cm, W. 47.6 cm, D. 90.8 cm; Upper floor, gallery 25; JE 62029;

Found in the antechamber, this chair is carved from cedar wood and partially gilded. The upper part shows a winged solar disc that is adorned by two cobras in gold leaf, which are fixed to the wood. On the sides are the king's cartouches. The main theme here is the god Heh, who is shown seated on the *nbw* sign of gold. He is holding two palm ribs and an *ankh* sign hangs from his arm. Over his head, is a solar disc flanked by two cobras.

The chair legs are of feline design with gilded claws, and typical of chairs in the New Kingdom Period. Between the legs, was a gilded *sematawy* symbol, representing the unity of Upper and Lower Egypt, which is now destroyed.

Heh was the god of infinity, who is represented as a kneeling man holding a palm rib, or alternatively, sometimes with a palm rib on his head. The palm rib is called *rnpt,* which means 'a year'. The word Heh means a million; he was the god of eternal life. Eternity was symbolised by the word *djet* as well; *djet* was static eternity, while Heh was dynamic eternity. Heh belonged to the Ogdood pantheon of Hermopolis, according to that theory of creation. Sometimes, he is represented holding a solar barque, lifting it to heaven at the end of its journey through the underworld.

Both sides of the chair show falcons, wearing the double crown of Upper and Lower Egypt, and representing the king himself.

84 & 85. Mirror box with god Heh

Wood, gold leaf; H. 26 cm, W. 14 cm; Upper floor, room 3; JE 62348;

This refined mirror case shows the god Heh as the main motif. He is represented in the above-mentioned pose, a kneeling man holding a palm rib and
flanked by two cartouches giving the names of the king. Above his head, is the
name *Neb kheperw re,* which is enclosed in an ornamented frame.

The mirror itself, probably made of silver, is now lost. It is thought to have
been taken by tomb robbers, who broke into the tomb to pilfer gold and other
valuables. Theban priests subsequently resealed the tomb.

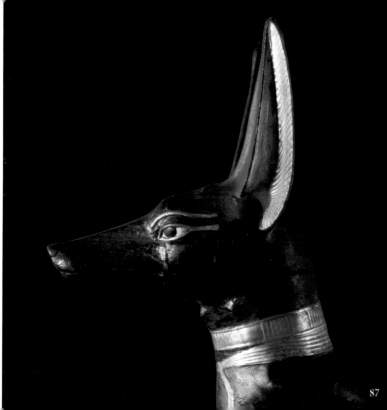

86 & 87. Anubis

Wood, stuccoed, gold, silver and stone; H. 118 cm, L. 270 cm, W. 52 cm;
Upper floor, gallery 9; JE 61444;

This statue of the jackal god Anubis was carved of wood painted black and partly covered with gold. It was discovered in the treasury room inside the tomb covered with a linen cloth. It surmounts a box that contained amulets, pectorals and cups. The box rests over a sledge, supplied with four poles that used to rest on shoulders of servants who carried it during the funeral procession of the king.

The perfect representation of the anatomy of the jackal is indeed so remarkable, reflecting a great artistic sense.

The jackal god Anubis was one of the most important funerary gods. He belonged to the mythical Osirian cycle. The black colour was associated with the fertile black soil of the Nile valley that was linked with the concept of rebirth. Anubis was the protector god of the necropolis, a guide for the dead, who also kept watch over the cemetery. His cult was assimilated with Osiris, as the one that wrapped the body of Osiris. Anubis, therefore, was closely connected to the mummification process. The epithets representing his funerary role were many: 'The Great God', 'The Foremost of the Westerners', 'The Foremost of the Divine Booth', 'He Who is Upon His Mountain', 'The Lord of the Sacred Land', 'The Master of the Necropolis', 'He Who is in the Mummy Wrapping', 'The Undertaker', 'He Who is in the Place of Embalmment'.

0 & 91. Ritual couch of Ammut

ilded wood; H. 134 cm, L. 236 cm, W. 126 cm; Upper floor, gallery 9;
E 61444;

This is one of three couches made of wood covered with a gold leaf. They
ere found in the antechamber in front of the entrance of the burial chamber.
hey represent the sacred animals hippopotamus, cow and the lioness.

Their height and form is symbolic and shows that they serve funerary func-
on; the king never used them in his actual life. They were of the traditional
yal funerary furniture as other couches of the same form and shape were
und in the tomb of Horemheb and others were represented in the tomb of
ng Ramsses III.

The three goddesses symbolize the idea of resurrection and protection in the
alm of the hereafter as the cow represents the goddess Mehet Weret the god-
ess who emerged from the primeval ocean Nun carrying the sun god Re. The
oness represents the goddess Mehet who causes the flood to be created every
ear thus symbolizing the idea of the rebirth for the king. The third represents
e goddess Nut that will take the deceased king in heaven in order to join the
ars that are reborn every night.

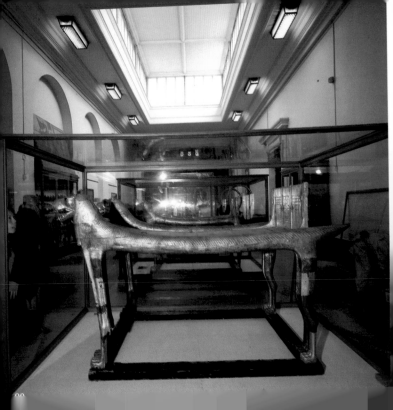

94 - 100. Painted chest

Stuccoed and painted wood; H. 44 cm, L. 61 cm, W. 43 cm;
Upper floor, gallery 20; JE 61467;

This superb wooden chest, which was discovered in the antechamber of the tomb, is in an excellent state of preservation. It was one of the chests used to store luxury items and the personal belongings of the deceased, such as papyrus sandals, a gilded headrest, ritual robes, scarves, belts and necklaces. Many other boxes and chests were found in the tomb, some were shrine-shaped, others had flat lids or double-pitched gable lids. The lid on this chest is secured with cords wound around large knobs.

The scenes on the sides are also framed by geometric motifs. Cartouches of the king are surmounted by two feathers and a solar disc; and the cartouche rest over the hieroglyph *nbw*, meaning gold. Also on the sides are symmetrical representations of the king as a sphinx, trampling over his enemies, which here include the Nubians and Asiatics, whom he crushes under his paws.

On the side of the lid is Tutankhamun's cartouche, which is protected by the solar disc, two cobra heads and two wings of vultures at the sides.

The front and rear sides of the chest (next page) are decorated with a battle scene showing the king's victories over his enemies. The scene on the front is surrounded by geometric and floral motifs. The king appears here on a much larger scale, dominating the scene; and is shown wearing the *kheperesh* Blue Crown, and riding in his chariot with horses, galloping. Holding the bow, he shoots arrows at his Asiatic enemies, who fall on the ground in confusion and disorder. Two fan bearers are shown walking behind him, and chariots of the army supporting the king follow close behind, represented with great discipline and order. Two protective vultures are hovering over the head of the king holding the *shen* sign of eternity and infinity; between them we see a solar disc with two heads of protective cobras. On the uppermost part of the chest, above the king himelf, is the sign *pt*, which means 'the sky', to show that the heavens are watching over the king. The rear side of the chest shows a similar battle scene against the Nubians.

Such battle scene postures had become the traditional theme for a victorious king since the time of Tuthmosis IV, and later found their place on the pylons and walls of temples, such as the battles of Ramsses II and Ramsses III.

The lid shows a hunting scene (next pages), which symbolises the victory of the king over the evil that would cause cosmic disorder. At the same time, hunting in the desert may well have been one of the royal hobbies that the king enjoyed in his free time.

In the hunting scene on the lid itself, the king and his companion are hunting with bows and arrows in their chariots. The king is shooting animals like gazelles, hyenas, ostriches and lions, which flee from him in confusion.

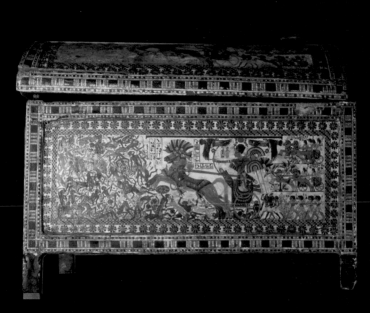

95

103 - 107. Ornamented chest

Wood, ebony; H. 48.5 cm, L. 72 cm, W. 53cm; Upper floor, gallery 25; JE 61477;

This outstanding shrine-shaped box is made of wood inlaid with ivory and ebony, lapis lazuli and carnelian. Ivory tusks had been split to make thin panels on the box. The lid design is framed by geometric patterns inlaid with lapis lazuli and carnelian, surrounding another frame of floral motifs, also inlaid with ivory and ebony, showing cornflowers and mandrakes as well as pomegranates. The side shows a desert hunting scene, where trained dogs, lions, and leopards attack antelopes, bulls and calves.

The lid on this chest shows the royal couple in a scene revealing intimacy and affection. The queen is represented in a wig that is surmounted by a perfumed wax cone, with two cobras at the sides, and a large pectoral. Her transparent, pleated, fluffy dress reveals details of her body. She is holding a bouquet of lotus flowers, papyrus stems and mandrakes, ready to present to the king, who is shown wearing a layered curly wig, a large pectoral covering his shoulders, as well as a short pleated kilt. His body is inclining forward as though he is talking to her and about to accept the bouquet she is holding. The scene is lifelike and naturalistic. Beneath it, servants are seen picking the flowers for the bouquet.

On the sides of the chest, another scene of the royal couple shows them sitting in a garden, in which there is a pond filled with fish. The king sits on a cushioned chair and his wife is sitting at his feet. Holding a bow and arrow to shoot birds, the queen is holding another arrow ready to hand to him, and a servant is carrying a bird and a fish that he has shot. The scene not only records one of the king's hobbies reveals the intimacy between the royal couple, but also signifies the king's triumph over the evils that would cause cosmic disorder.

103

106

110 & 111. Ivory headrest with Shu

Ivory; H. 17.5 cm, W. 29.2 cm; Upper floor, gallery 9; JE 62020;

This *wrs* headrest was sculpted out of solid ivory, and consists of three parts the curved neckpiece, the column and the base. Originally it was also provided with a cushion. Not only was such a headrest used during sleep, but also had religious significance in the burial.

The column here is in the form of the god Shu, the god of air who would carry the king's head and raise it to heaven, as the one who had raised the goddess Nut to the sky, away from Geb the god of earth. Shu is shown as a man wearing a straight wig and a pleated kilt. The two lion gods at the right and left sides are together the god Akr, who is identified with the eastern and western horizons. They support the rise of the sun between them, representing the sun of 'yesterday and tomorrow', thereby symbolising eternity. This imagery signifies that the deceased king would be raised to the heavens, to be reborn and rejuvenated, like the sun that rises in the eastern horizon each day. In addition the scene indicates that the head of the deceased would remain raised, as the sun rises eternally. At the same time, the head would not be separated from the mummy, as mentioned in Chapter 166 of the 'Book of the Dead'.

Several other headrests were found in the Tomb of Tutankhamun, made of faience or ivory in the form of a folding stool.

Headrests had been buried in tombs since the Old Kingdom period, and the ancient Egyptians sometimes made small models of them, to use as protective amulets. The actual headrests were made of various materials such as wood, granite or alabaster as well as ivory. Funerary amulets were made of hematite.

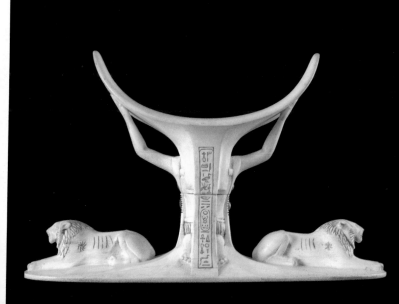

111

113. Lion unguent container

Alabaster, gold and ivory; H. 60 cm, W. 19.8 cm; Upper floor, gallery 20;
JE 62114;

This perfume container is sculpted in the form of a standing lion, which raises one leg as though greeting the viewer, and is placing the paw of another leg on the sign sa, which was one of the protective amulets. A lotus flower graces the top of the piece, as one of the symbols of rebirth and resurrection. The eyes of the lion are covered with gold leaf, and the tongue and teeth are carved of ivory, and inlaid. On the lion's chest are the cartouches of the king and queen. The base of the container is formed like a lattice type stand.

The lion is sometimes represented as the god Re himself, as in Chapter 62 of the 'Book of the Dead', which says 'I am he who crosses the sky, I am the lion of Re'. The two lion gods called Akr appear again here.

Perfume and unguent containers and jars were among the customary funerary equipment to be supplied for the dead as part of a proper burial, and to assure his well being in the afterlife. The preparation of unguents and perfumes was performed under the supervision of the *imy-is* or the *imy-khnet* priest.

Seven kinds of oils were placed in vases to go into the tombs. Some of the vases were amphora shaped, and others had a piriform body and a flat cylindrical mouth, or were cylindrical with splayed foot and conical mouth. In addition, some took on the form of a pitcher with one handle.

As well as vases containing perfume, slabs of alabaster were also used as receptacles. Measuring about 5.5 by 2.5 inches, they comprise seven circular hollows into which drops of perfume were poured. The names of the seven oils were inscribed on these slabs.

The perfume deity was the god Nefertum, son of god Ptah, the god of Memphis. He was known as 'the lord of perfumes'.

115. Calcite boat in a tank

Alabaster, gold, H. 37 cm, W. 58 cm; Upper floor, gallery 20; JE 62120;

This impressive artefact was sculpted of translucent alabaster stone, and found in the annex of the tomb. It was probably a decorative piece, a case of 'art for the art itself', as its function has not been determined with any certainty.

The boat is decorated with the heads of gazelles, which were supplied with real horns. Their necks are adorned with gilded collars. Two female dwarves are sailing the boat, one sitting at the prow, holding a lotus flower, and the other standing on the stern. The object she formerly held is now lost. Both dwarves are represented with curly wigs, and are naked, except for their bracelets and armbands. The one on the prow is wearing a gold earring. The boat has a central cabin, surrounded by four columns that support a canopy. Both cabin and canopy are ornamented with cavetto cornices; and the columns boast papy-

rus capitals, which emerge from lotus flowers. Partially, painted and gilded, the boat rests on a pedestal in the middle of a basin. The basin's outer surface is decorated by floral and geometric motifs.

117. Calcite ibex vase

Alabaster; H. 27.5, L. 38.5, W. 18.5 cm; Upper floor, gallery 20; JE 62122;

This alabaster vase, discovered in the tomb annex, is one of the innovative forms of perfume and unguent containers in the collection of Tutankhamun's funerary equipage. The ibex horn is actual, adding life and an air of realism to the piece. Originally, there were two horns, but one is lost. The facial features and the eyes are painted black, and the eyes themselves are inlaid with translucent rock crystal. The tongue of the ibex is carved of ivory, stained red and inlaid over the alabaster. The cartouche on the body of the ibex, contains the name *Nebkheperwre*, which is one of Tutankhamun's names, and this is surmounted by a solar disc flanked by two feathers.

120 & 121. Alabaster perfume vessel

Alabaster; H. 70.5 cm, W. 36 cm; Upper floor, gallery 20, JE 62114;

This remarkable alabaster perfume vessel was found in the burial chamber between the first and second shrines that housed the king's sarcophagus and the royal anthropoid coffins. Sculpted of four alabaster pieces that were fixed together, it features the *sematawy* sign. This sign, which indicates the unification of the two lands, that is, the north and south of Egypt, appears frequently on the sides of royal thrones throughout Egyptian history.

The two figures flanking the container, represent the god of the Nile, who ties the papyrus plant, signifying the north, and the lotus plant, symbolising the south of the country. During the months of the year when there was no inundation, the Egyptians called the Nile *itrw*. During the inundation season, they called it Hapy, who was deified and represented as a man with pendulous breasts and a prominent belly. In some representations, the body is covered with wavy blue lines, representing water.

The cartouches of the king and queen are inscribed on the container, and the upper part shows two cobras. The one on the right is wearing the *hedjet* White Crown of Upper Egypt and the other wears the *desheret* Red Crown of Lower Egypt. The flat rim of the container is surmounted by a vulture, which spreads its wings in a protective manner to guard the figure of the king that, most likely, formed the stopper on the rim.

The cartouches of the king appear again on the base that supports the container. Two falcons with outspread wings surround the cartouches. Above them are solar discs and the sign *nbw*, meaning 'gold'. This scene signifies the mythical victory of god Horus over his enemy Seth, who, as the god of the city Ombos, is identified as the sign of gold.

123. Ceremonial chariot

Wood, gold Leaf, semi-precious stones and glass; H. 118 cm, L. 250 cm;
Upper floor, gallery 13; JE 61989;

This chariot is one of four that were found dismantled in the antechamber of the tomb. They were probably dismantled to allow them to pass through the tomb's narrow entrance, and most likely remained in pieces due to a lack of space inside. Chariots were sometimes taken into the tomb intact during funerals or were first dismantled then taken to the tomb in pieces. The dismantled chariot, moreover, represented death, due to its lack of dynamism.

The pieces were heaped up in confusion, as tomb robbers had broken into the tomb to steal gold. Theban priests subsequently resealed the tomb, however. Once reassembled, the chariots proved to be in an excellent state of preservation. They are made of wood covered with gold.

As Tutankhamun's reign was a peaceful one, and he was not one of the warrior kings, his chariots were used in civil life: for hunting, parades and rides. However, his military general Horemheb, who later became king, did lead a campaign in Asia in order to regain territory overrun by the Hittites. These adventures are illustrated alongside the royal cartouches, and the king, in sphinx form, tramples over the two rows of Negroes alternating with Asiatic enemies who are tied together with a rope. The falcon standing over the figure of an enemy, is a symbolic representation of the king's victory.

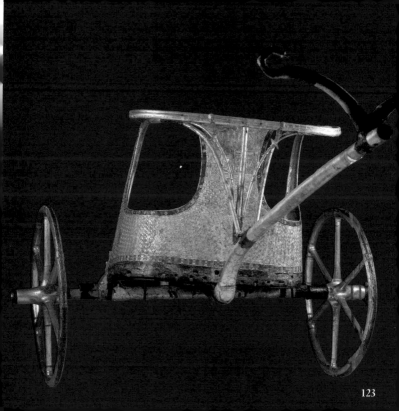

125 - 131. Accessories of the cermonial chariot

Wood, gold Leaf, semi-precious stones and glass;
Upper floor, gallery 13;

These accessories of the chariots were the stirrups, spindles and the saddle as well as the blinders that were used to cover the eyes of horses for high jumps. War chariots, in addition, had quivers attached to the sides, for holding bows and arrows. The blinders of the ceremonial chariot of the king feature the *udjat* eye of Horus and lotus flower. The decoration also shows two heads of Bes, a deity who protected against terror and snakebites as well as scorpions. In addition it was his role to watch over childbirth.

In the New Kingdom Period, the scene of the king riding his chariot, poised with bow and arrow ready to attack his enemies, became the conventional scene for a king victorious over the real enemy, which was the evil causing cosmic chaos, represented here by the animals.

Chariots had arrived in Egypt by the time of the Hyksos domination, but their origin is difficult to determine with certainty. A considerable number were imported from Northern Syria and Mesopotamia. They were made of wood, ornamented with gold and silver. The chariots are constructed of a light wooden semicircular and open-backed framework, furnished with an axle and a pair of either four or six-spoke wheels. A long pole attached to the axle by leather straps enabled the chariot to be drawn by a pair of horses, or alternatively, oxen or mules.

129

133. Game boards

Wood, ivory, bronze; H. 48 cm, L. 72 cm, W. 53 cm;

Upper floor, gallery 35; JE 61477;

Manufactured of wood and ivory, these game boards were discovered in the annex to the antechamber. The largest one is placed on feline legs and fixed to a sledge. The variety of the boards and their differing sizes indicate that this was the king's favourite game. There is even a pocket sized one for him to take along on trips and outings.

This game is called *senet*, which means passing. The gaming board consists of thirty squares divided into three rows of ten. The players threw little sticks or dice to take their moves. By blocking or removing the opponent's pieces, a player aimed to remove all his pieces from the board first. The *senet* game was one of the symbolic requirements of the funerary equipment for tombs.

In Chapter 17 of the 'Book of the Coming Forth by Day' ('The Book of the Dead'), the deceased is demanded to play this game against an invisible opponent, which could be fate or death itself. Winning assured success in overcoming any obstacles that might hinder his way towards resurrection and immortality. The game appeared as early as the Archaic Period and appears in the mural scenes on the 'mastabas' in Giza and Sakkara from the Old Kingdom Period.

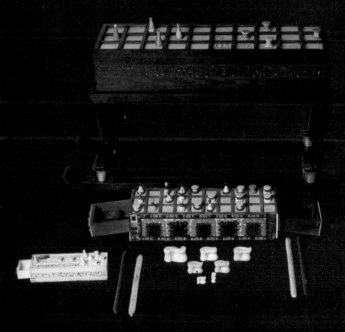

In addition, one of the most famous and best preserved scenes in the Tomb of Queen Nefertary, wife of Ramsess II, in the Valley of the Queens in Thebes, shows the queen playing the *senet* game. It was a scene that reappeared at various times throughout Egyptian history, for example, in the Tomb of Padiwsir (Petosiris) in Tuna el Gebel near Minya, which dates from the third century B.C.

The ancient Egyptians had other board games, such as the *men*, which means the endurance game. This one required two players and involved a long, narrow board that was divided into thirteen sections. In addition, there was the *mehen* game, which means 'serpent', and was played on a round slotted board in the form of a coiled snake. This game could be played by up to six people.

135. Boat with a sail

Wood, linen; Upper floor, gallery 20; JE 61239;

One of thirty five models of boats discovered in the treasury and the annex to the antechamber, this one is carved of solid wood, covered with gesso and painted. It has a central cabin, with a stair for access. The kiosks on the stern and prow, consist of an open canopy carried by four columns. The one on the right is decorated by a bull, and the other features a walking sphinx. The sail and cords are made of linen and there are two oars. Models of boats were believed to provide the deceased with a means of transport in the Nile of the hereafter. Two kinds were usually placed in the tomb, one intended for sailing

south with the prevailing wind, and the other for rowing downstream with the water current, to the north.

Actual funerary boats were used to cross from the east to the west of the Nile, either heading to the embalmment house, or for burial in the necropolis. These boats were used to transport the deceased, as the Nile provided the easiest and the most direct route.

Boats were also used for pilgrimages to religious sites like Abydos and Busiris. The several types included the *neshmt,* used for pilgrimage, and the simple papyrus skiffs.

137. A barge

Wood, gold leaf; Upper floor, gallery 20; JE 61330;

Carved of wood, covered with gesso and painted, this transport barge was discovered in Tutankhamun's tomb treasury. It has two steering oars but no sail. Steps lead to the central cabin, and the boat has kiosks on the stern and prow like the one above. Each kiosk consists of an open canopy supported by four columns. The one on the right is decorated with a bull, and the other features a walking sphinx.

Several boats were used together for funerals and sometimes a procession of boats crossed the Nile to go to the necropolis. Probably, there was a ready to go-fleet in Thebes that was rented for both funerals and pilgrimages.

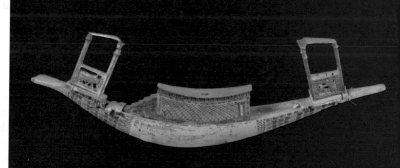

139. Shield

Gilded wood; H. 88 cm, W. 55 cm; Upper floor, gallery 45; JE 61576;

This shield was carved of wood covered with a gold leave. Its filigree technique indicates its function; it was a ceremonial shield used only during celebrations and ceremonies. The uppermost part shows the winged solar disc symbolizing the theme of victory. The king is shown raising the sword of victory in one hand and the other hand holds a panther by the tail which demands a great vigor and determination. This is a traditional pose for the victorious king who overcomes his enemies represented as savage and wild animals. Behind him, we see a vulture spreading her wings protecting him; the vulture wears the crown of Upper Egypt and stands over papyrus plants symbolizing Lower Egypt.

The lower part shows the mountains symbolizing foreign countries as though it represents the victory of the king over forign enemies. One of the King's duties was winning a victory over enemies symbolizing fighting the evil in the world which would cause cosmic disorder.

The most common material for real shields in ancient Egypt was cow hide, and the ancient word for shield, *ikm*, is typically determined with a sign identified as a cow hide. In later periods shields were covered with copper or bronze. They varied in size, some being small and easily portable and others long enough to protect a standing man.

139

141. Leopard head

Gilded wood, quartz and glas paste; H. 16.5 cm; Upper floor, gallery 8;

This head of a leopard made of wood covered with a gold layer used to be fixed over a real leopard skin that used to form the traditional garment for a *sm* priest which is one of the high rank priests.

It is represented with fine features and shows the name of the king in his cartouche over the forehead. The eye lines are inlayed with lapis lazuli and the eyes themselves are inlayed with white quartz and rock crystal.

The priesthood had special emblems and garments such as shaved heads and white linen dresses. While leopard skin was used to symbolize high rank of priesthood or prophets of temples of gods.

Kings used to acquire leopard skin to symbolize their role for the gods. The first time a king appeared wearing the leopard skin was king Amenemhat III of the 12th Dynasty.

143. Tutankhamen as god Khonsu

Granite; H. 152 cm; Grround floor, room 12; CG 39488;

This granite statue of King Tutankhamun was sculpted of granite and found in Karnak. It shows the king with a lock of hair at the side of his head, and a cobra over his forehead. He is holding the *djed* pillar, the *nekhekh* flail and the *heka* crook; and wearing the large pectoral and its counterpoise, all these emblems signify god Khonsu.

As member of the Theban Triad worshipped at Karnak, Khonsu was the son of the god Amun and the goddess Mut. Khonsu was a moon god whose name means 'the wanderer'.

In addition, he was worshipped as the son of Sobek and Hathor at Kom Ombo, where he was associated with Horus, and called Khonsu-Hor.

Equipment

I photographed all pictures of this book with my Hasselblad. For portraits and statues I used the Hasselblad 500 CM and 501CM with Sonar 150 mm lens. For close-ups I used the Macro Planar 120 mm lens and for greater magnification Macro Planar 135 mm lens with bellows. The normal lenses used were the Planar 80 mm and 100 mm lenses. For wide angle pictures I used the Hasselblad SWC/M with the Biogon 38 mm lens. And Fuji Provia 100 ASA film has been used in all cases.

The various stages of printing were carried out at my printing house 'Farid Atiya Press'. Colour seperation and image setting we did with the 'superb' Hell drum scanner. This heavy duty classical machine gave excellent results, and cannot be compared with the modern 'digital photography'. Kodak Polychrome image setting films were used. The offset printing we did with the Heidelberg SORSZ machine. Hartmann printing ink and varnish were used.

Farid Atiya